Economic Depressions:
Their Cause and Cure

Economic Depressions:
Their Cause and Cure

Murray N. Rothbard

MISES INSTITUTE

© 2009 by the Ludwig von Mises Institute and published under the Creative Commons Attribution License 3.0.
http://creativecommons.org/licenses/by/3.0/

Ludwig von Mises Institute
518 West Magnolia Avenue
Auburn, Alabama 36832
www.mises.org

Large Print Edition published 2012 by Skyler J. Collins. Visit: www.skylerjcollins.com.

Cover image by StockFreeImages.com

ISBN-13: 978-1479259120
ISBN-10: 1479259128

...banks would never be able to expand credit in concert were it not for the intervention and encouragement of government.

— Murray N. Rothbard

Economic Depressions:
Their Cause and Cure

WE LIVE in a world of euphemism. Undertakers have become "morticians," press agents are now "public relations counsellors" and janitors have all been transformed into "superintendents." In every walk of life, plain facts have been wrapped in cloudy camouflage.

No less has this been true of economics. In the old days, we used to suffer

This essay was originally published as a minibook by the Constitutional Alliance of Lansing, Michigan, 1969. It is also included in *The Austrian Theory of the Trade Cycle and Other Essays*, Richard M. Ebeling, ed. (Auburn, Ala.: Ludwig von Mises Institute, 2006).

nearly periodic economic crises, the sudden onset of which was called a "panic," and the lingering trough period after the panic was called "depression."

The most famous depression in modern times, of course, was the one that began in a typical financial panic in 1929 and lasted until the advent of World War II. After the disaster of 1929, economists and politicians resolved that this must never happen again. The easiest way of succeeding at this resolve was, simply to define "depressions" out of existence. From that point on, America was to suffer no further depressions. For when the next sharp depression came along, in 1937–38, the economists simply refused to use the dread name, and came up with a new, much softer-sounding word: "recession." From that point on, we have been through quite a few recessions, but not a single depression.

But pretty soon the word "recession" also became too harsh for the delicate sensibilities of the American public. It now seems that we had our last recession in 1957–58. For since then, we have only had "downturns," or, even better, "slowdowns," or "sidewise movements." So be of good cheer; from now on, depressions and even recessions have been outlawed by the semantic fiat of economists; from now on, the worst that can possibly happen to us are "slowdowns." Such are the wonders of the "New Economics."

For 30 years, our nation's economists have adopted the view of the business cycle held by the late British economist, John Maynard Keynes, who created the Keynesian, or the "New," Economics in his book, *The General Theory of Employment, Interest, and Money*, published in 1936. Beneath their diagrams, mathematics, and inchoate jargon, the attitude of Keynesians toward booms and bust is simplicity, even naivete, itself. If there is inflation, then the cause is supposed to be "excessive spending" on the part of the public; the alleged cure is for the government, the self-appointed stabilizer and regulator of the nation's economy, to step in and force people to spend less, "sopping up their excess purchasing power" through increased taxation. If there is a recession, on the other hand, this has been caused by insufficient private spending, and the cure now is for the government to increase its own spending, preferably through deficits, thereby adding to the nation's aggregate spending stream.

The idea that increased government spending or easy money is "good for business" and that budget cuts or harder money is "bad" permeates even the most conservative newspapers and magazines. These journals will also take for granted that it is the sacred task of the federal government to steer the economic system on the narrow road between the abysses of depression on the one hand and inflation on the other, for the free-market economy is supposed to be ever liable to succumb to one of these evils.

All current schools of economists have the same attitude. Note, for example, the viewpoint of Dr. Paul W. McCracken, the incoming chairman of President Nixon's Council of Economic Advisers. In an interview with the *New York Times* shortly after taking office (January 24, 1969), Dr. McCracken asserted that one of the major economic problems facing the new administration is "how you cool down this inflationary economy without at the same time tripping off unacceptably high levels of unemployment. In other words, if the only thing we want to do is cool off the inflation, it could be done. But our social tolerances on unemployment are narrow." And again: "I think we have to feel our way along here. We don't really have much experience in trying to cool an economy in orderly fashion. We slammed on the brakes in 1957, but, of course, we got substantial slack in the economy."

Note the fundamental attitude of Dr. McCracken toward the economy—remarkable only in that it is shared by almost all economists of the present day. The economy is treated as a potentially workable, but always troublesome and recalcitrant patient, with a continual tendency to hive off into greater inflation or unemployment. The function of the government is to be the wise old manager and physician, ever watchful, ever tinkering to keep the economic patient in good working order. In any case, here the economic patient is clearly supposed to be the subject, and the government as "physician" the master.

It was not so long ago that this kind of attitude and policy was called "socialism"; but we live in a world of euphemism, and now we call it by far less harsh labels, such as "moderation" or "enlightened free enterprise." We live and learn.

What, then, are the causes of periodic depressions? Must we always remain agnostic about the causes of booms and busts? Is it really true that business cycles are rooted deep within the free-market economy, and that therefore some form of government planning is needed if we wish to keep the economy within some kind of stable bounds? Do booms and then busts just simply happen, or does one phase of the cycle flow logically from the other?

The currently fashionable attitude toward the business cycle stems, actually, from Karl Marx. Marx saw that, before the Industrial Revolution in approximately the late eighteenth century, there were no regularly recurring booms and depressions. There would be a sudden economic crisis whenever some king made war or confiscated the property of his subject; but there was no sign of the peculiarly modern phenomena of general and fairly regular swings in business fortunes, of expansions and contractions. Since these cycles also appeared on the scene at about the same time as modern industry, Marx concluded that business cycles were an inherent feature of the capitalist market economy. All the various current schools of economic thought, regardless of their other differences and the different causes that they attribute to the cycle, agree on this vital point: That these business cycles originate somewhere deep within the free-market economy. The market economy is to blame. Karl Marx believed that the periodic depressions would get worse and worse, until the masses would be moved to revolt and destroy the system, while the modern economists believe that the government can successfully stabilize depressions and the cycle. But all parties agree that the fault lies deep within the market economy and that if anything can save the day, it must be some form of massive government intervention.

There are, however, some critical problems in the assumption that the market economy is the culprit. For "general economic theory" teaches us that supply and demand always tend to be in equilibrium in the market and that therefore prices of products as well as of the factors that contribute to production are always tending toward some equilibrium point. Even though changes of data, which are always taking place, prevent equilibrium from ever being reached, there is nothing in the general theory of the market system that would account for regular and recurring boom-and-bust phases of the business cycle. Modern economists "solve" this problem by simply keeping their general price and market theory and their business cycle theory in separate, tightly-sealed compartments, with never the twain meeting, much less integrated with each other. Economists, unfortunately, have forgotten that there is only one economy and therefore only one integrated economic theory. Neither economic life nor the structure of theory can or should be in watertight compartments; our knowledge of the economy is either one integrated whole or it is nothing. Yet most economists are content to apply totally separate and, indeed, mutually exclusive, theories for general price analysis and for business cycles. They cannot be genuine economic scientists so long as they are content to keep operating in this primitive way.

But there are still graver problems with the currently fashionable approach. Economists also do not see one particularly critical problem because they do not bother to square their business cycle and general price theories: the peculiar breakdown of the entrepreneurial function at times of economic crisis and depression. In the market economy, one of the most vital functions of the businessman is to be an "entrepreneur," a man who invests in productive methods, who buys equipment and hires labor to produce something which he is not sure will reap him any return. In short, the entrepreneurial function is the function of forecasting the uncertain future. Before embarking on any investment or line of production, the entrepreneur, or "enterpriser," must estimate present and future costs and future revenues and therefore estimate whether and how much profits he will earn from the investment. If he forecasts well and significantly better than his business competitors, he will reap profits from his investment. The better his forecasting, the higher the profits he will earn. If, on the other hand, he is a poor forecaster and overestimates the demand for his product, he will suffer losses and pretty soon be forced out of the business.

The market economy, then, is a profit-and-loss economy, in which the acumen and ability of business entrepreneurs is gauged by the profits and losses they reap. The market economy, moreover, contains a built-in mechanism, a kind of natural selection, that ensures the survival and the flourishing of the superior forecaster and the weeding-out of the inferior ones. For the more profits reaped by the better forecasters, the greater become their business responsibilities, and the more they will have available to invest in the productive system. On the other hand, a few years of making losses will drive the poorer forecasters and entrepreneurs out of business altogether and push them into the ranks of salaried employees.

If, then, the market economy has a built-in natural selection mechanism for good entrepreneurs, this means that, generally, we would expect not many business firms to be making losses. And, in fact, if we look around at the economy on an average day or year, we will find that losses are not very widespread. But, in that case, the odd fact that needs explaining is this: How is it that, periodically, in times of the onset of recessions and especially in steep depressions, the business world suddenly experiences a massive cluster of severe losses? A moment arrives when business firms, previously highly astute entrepreneurs in their ability to make profits and avoid losses, suddenly and dismayingly find themselves, almost all of them, suffering severe and unaccountable losses? How come? Here is a momentous fact that any theory of depressions must explain. An explanation such as "underconsumption"—a drop in total consumer spending—is not sufficient, for one thing, because what needs to be explained is why businessmen, able to forecast all manner of previous economic changes and developments, proved themselves totally and catastrophically unable to forecast this alleged drop in consumer demand. Why this sudden failure in forecasting ability?

An adequate theory of depressions, then, must account for the tendency of the economy to move through successive booms and busts, showing no sign of settling into any sort of smoothly moving, or quietly progressive, approximation of an equilibrium situation. In particular, a theory of depression must account for the mammoth cluster of errors which appears swiftly and suddenly at a moment of economic crisis, and lingers through the depression period until recovery. And there is a third universal fact that a theory of the cycle must account for. Invariably, the booms and busts are much more intense and severe in the "capital goods industries"—the industries making machines and equipment, the ones producing industrial raw materials or constructing industrial plants—than in the industries making consumers' goods. Here is another fact of business cycle life that must be explained—and obviously can't be explained by such theories of depression as the popular underconsumption doctrine: That consumers aren't spending enough on consumer goods. For if insufficient spending is the culprit, then how is it that retail sales are the last and the least to fall in any depression, and that depression *really* hits such industries as machine tools, capital equipment, construction, and raw materials? Conversely, it is these industries that really take off in the inflationary boom phases of the business cycle, and not those businesses serving the consumer. An adequate theory of the business cycle, then, must also explain the far greater intensity of booms and busts in the non-consumer goods, or "producers' goods," industries.

Fortunately, a correct theory of depression and of the business cycle *does* exist, even though it is universally neglected in present-day economics. It, too, has a long tradition in economic thought. This theory began with the eighteenth century Scottish philosopher and economist David Hume, and with the eminent early nineteenth century English classical economist David Ricardo. Essentially, these theorists saw that another crucial institution had developed in the mid-eighteenth century, alongside the industrial system. This was the institution of banking, with its capacity to expand credit and the money supply (first, in the form of paper money, or bank notes, and later in the form of demand deposits, or checking accounts, that are instantly redeemable in cash at the banks). It was the operations of these commercial banks which, these economists saw, held the key to the mysterious recurrent cycles of expansion and contraction, of boom and bust, that had puzzled observers since the mid-eighteenth century.

The Ricardian analysis of the business cycle went something as follows: The natural moneys emerging as such on the world free market are useful commodities, generally gold and silver. If money were confined simply to these commodities, then the economy would work in the aggregate as it does in particular markets: A smooth adjustment of supply and demand, and therefore no cycles of boom and bust. But the injection of bank credit adds another crucial and disruptive element. For the banks expand credit and therefore bank money in the form of notes or deposits which are theoretically redeemable on demand in gold, but in practice clearly are not. For example, if a bank has 1,000 ounces of gold in its vaults, and it issues instantly redeemable warehouse receipts for 2,500 ounces of gold, then it clearly has issued 1,500 ounces more than it can possibly redeem. But so long as there is no concerted "run" on the bank to cash in these receipts, its warehouse-receipts function on the market as equivalent to gold, and therefore the bank has been able to expand the money supply of the country by 1,500 gold ounces.

The banks, then, happily begin to expand credit, for the more they expand credit the greater will be their profits. This results in the expansion of the money supply within a country, say England. As the supply of paper and bank money in England increases, the money incomes and expenditures of Englishmen rise, and the increased money bids up prices of English goods. The result is inflation and a boom within the country. But this inflationary boom, while it proceeds on its merry way, sows the seeds of its own demise. For as English money supply and incomes increase, Englishmen proceed to purchase more goods from abroad. Furthermore, as English prices go up, English goods begin to lose their competitiveness with the products of other countries which have not inflated, or have been inflating to a lesser degree. Englishmen begin to buy less at home and more abroad, while foreigners buy less in England and more at home; the result is a deficit in the English balance of payments, with English exports falling sharply behind imports. But if imports exceed exports, this means that money must flow out of England to foreign countries. And what money will this be? Surely not English bank notes or deposits, for Frenchmen or Germans or Italians have little or no interest in keeping their funds locked up in English banks. These foreigners will therefore take their bank notes and deposits and present them to the English banks for redemption in gold—and gold will be the type of money that will tend to flow persistently out of the country as the English inflation proceeds on its way. But this means that English bank credit money will be, more and more, pyramiding on top of a dwindling gold base in the English bank vaults. As the boom proceeds, our hypothetical bank will expand its warehouse receipts issued from, say 2,500 ounces to 4,000 ounces, while its gold base dwindles to, say, 800. As this process intensifies, the banks will eventually become frightened. For the banks, after all, are obligated to redeem their liabilities in cash, and their cash is flowing out rapidly as their liabilities pile up. Hence, the banks will eventually lose their nerve, stop their credit expansion, and in order to save themselves, contract their bank loans outstanding. Often, this retreat is precipitated by bankrupting runs on the banks touched off by the public, who had also been getting increasingly nervous about the ever more shaky condition of the nation's banks.

The bank contraction reverses the economic picture; contraction and bust follow boom. The banks pull in their horns, and businesses suffer as the pressure mounts for debt repayment and contraction. The fall in the supply of bank money, in turn, leads to a general fall in English prices. As money supply and incomes fall, and

English prices collapse, English goods become relatively more attractive in terms of foreign products, and the balance of payments reverses itself, with exports exceeding imports. As gold flows into the country, and as bank money contracts on top of an expanding gold base, the condition of the banks becomes much sounder.

This, then, is the meaning of the depression phase of the business cycle. Note that it is a phase that comes out of, and inevitably comes out of, the preceding expansionary boom. It is the preceding inflation that makes the depression phase necessary. We can see, for example, that the depression is the process by which the market economy adjusts, throws off the excesses and distortions of the previous inflationary boom, and reestablishes a sound economic condition. The depression is the unpleasant but necessary reaction to the distortions and excesses of the previous boom.

Why, then, does the next cycle begin? Why do business cycles tend to be recurrent and continuous? Because when the banks have pretty well recovered, and are in a sounder condition, they are then in a confident position to proceed to their natural path of bank credit expansion, and the next boom proceeds on its way, sowing the seeds for the next inevitable bust.

But if banking is the cause of the business cycle, aren't the banks also a part of the private market economy, and can't we therefore say that the free market is *still* the culprit, if only in the banking segment of that free market? The answer is No, for the banks, for one thing, would never be able to expand credit in concert were it not for the intervention and encouragement of government. For if banks were truly competitive, any expansion of credit by one bank would quickly pile up the debts of that bank in its competitors, and its competitors would quickly call upon the expanding bank for redemption in cash. In short, a bank's rivals will call upon it for redemption in gold or cash in the same way as do foreigners, except that the process is much faster and would nip any incipient inflation in the bud before it got started. Banks can only expand comfortably in unison when a Central Bank exists, essentially a governmental bank, enjoying a monopoly of government business, and a privileged position imposed by government over the entire banking system. It is only when central banking got established that the banks were able to expand for any length of time and the familiar business cycle got underway in the modern world.

The central bank acquires its control over the banking system by such governmental measures as: Making its own liabilities legal tender for all debts and receivable in taxes; granting the central bank monopoly of the issue of bank *notes*, as contrasted to deposits (in England the Bank of England, the governmentally established central bank, had a legal monopoly of bank notes in the London area); or through the outright forcing of banks to use the central bank as their client for keeping their reserves of cash (as in the United States and its Federal Reserve System). Not that the banks complain about this intervention; for it is the establishment of central banking that makes long-term bank credit expansion possible, since the expansion of Central Bank notes provides added cash reserves for the entire banking system and permits all the commercial banks to expand their credit together. Central banking works like a cozy compulsory bank cartel to expand the banks' liabilities; and the banks are now able to expand on a larger base of cash in the form of central bank notes as well as gold.

So now we see, at last, that the business cycle is brought about, not by any mysterious failings of the free market economy, but quite the opposite: By systematic intervention by government in the market process. Government intervention brings about bank expansion and inflation, and, when the inflation comes to an end, the subsequent depression-adjustment comes into play.

The Ricardian theory of the business cycle grasped the essentials of a correct cycle theory: The recurrent nature of the phases of the cycle, depression as adjustment intervention in the market rather than from the free-market economy. But two problems were as yet unexplained: Why the sudden cluster of business error, the sudden failure of the entrepreneurial function, and why the vastly greater fluctuations in the producers' goods than in the consumers' goods industries? The Ricardian theory only explained movements in the price level, in general business; there was no hint of explanation of the vastly different reactions in the capital and consumers' goods industries.

The correct and fully developed theory of the business cycle was finally discovered and set forth by the Austrian economist Ludwig von Mises, when he was a professor at the University of Vienna. Mises developed hints of his solution to the vital problem of the business cycle in his monumental *Theory of Money and Credit*, published in 1912, and still, nearly 60 years later, the best book on the theory of money and banking. Mises developed his cycle theory during the 1920s, and it was brought to the English-speaking world by Mises's leading follower, Friedrich A. von Hayek, who came from Vienna to teach at the London School of Economics in the early 1930s, and who published, in German and in English, two books which applied and elaborated the Mises cycle theory: *Monetary Theory and the Trade Cycle*, and *Prices and Production*. Since Mises and Hayek were Austrians, and also since they were in the tradition of the great nineteenth-century Austrian economists, this theory has become known in the literature as the "Austrian" (or the "monetary over-investment") theory of the business cycle.

Building on the Ricardians, on general "Austrian" theory, and on his own creative genius, Mises developed the following theory of the business cycle:

Without bank credit expansion, supply and demand tend to be equilibrated through the free price system, and no cumulative booms or busts can then develop. But then government through its central bank stimulates bank credit expansion by expanding central bank liabilities and therefore the cash reserves of all the nation's commercial banks. The banks then proceed to expand credit and hence the nation's money supply in the form of check deposits. As the Ricardians saw, this expansion of bank money drives up the prices of goods and hence causes inflation. But, Mises showed, it does something else, and something even more sinister. Bank credit expansion, by pouring new loan funds into the business world, artificially lowers the rate of interest in the economy below its free market level.

On the free and unhampered market, the interest rate is determined purely by the "time-preferences" of all the individuals that make up the market economy. For the essence of a loan is that a "present good" (money which can be used at present) is being exchanged for a "future good" (an IOU which can only be used at some point in the future). Since people always prefer money right now to the present prospect of getting the same amount of money some time in the future, the present good always commands a premium in the market over the future. This premium is the interest rate, and its height will vary according to the degree to which people prefer the present to the future, i.e., the degree of their time-preferences.

People's time-preferences also determine the extent to which people will save and invest, as compared to how much they will consume. If people's time-preferences should fall, i.e., if their degree of preference for present over future falls, then people will tend to consume less now and save and invest more; at the same time, and for the same reason, the rate of interest, the rate of time-discount, will also fall. Economic growth comes about largely as the result of falling rates of time-preference, which lead to an increase in the proportion of saving and investment to consumption, and also to a falling rate of interest.

But what happens when the rate of interest falls, not because of lower time-preferences and higher savings, but from government interference that promotes the expansion of bank credit? In other words, if the rate of interest falls artificially, due to intervention, rather than naturally, as a result of changes in the valuations and preferences of the consuming public?

What happens is trouble. For businessmen, seeing the rate of interest fall, react as they always would and must to such a change of market signals: They invest more in capital and producers' goods. Investments, particularly in lengthy and time-consuming projects, which previously looked unprofitable now seem profitable, because of the fall of the interest charge. In short, businessmen react as they would react if savings had *genuinely* increased: They expand their investment in durable equipment, in capital goods, in industrial raw material, in construction as compared to their direct production of consumer goods.

Businesses, in short, happily borrow the newly expanded bank money that is coming to them at cheaper rates; they use the money to invest in capital goods, and eventually this money gets paid out in higher rents to land, and higher wages to workers in the capital goods industries. The increased business demand bids up labor costs, but businesses think they can pay these higher costs because they have been fooled by the government-and-bank intervention in the loan market and its decisively important tampering with the interest-rate signal of the marketplace.

The problem comes as soon as the workers and landlords—largely the former, since most gross business income is paid out in wages—begin to spend the new bank money that they have received in the form of higher wages. For the time-preferences of the public have not *really* gotten lower; the public doesn't *want* to save more than it has. So the workers set about to consume most of their new income, in short to reestablish the old consumer/saving proportions. This means that they redirect the spending back to the consumer goods industries, and they don't save and invest enough to buy the newly-produced machines, capital equipment, industrial raw materials, etc. This all reveals itself as a sudden sharp and continuing depression in the *producers' goods* industries. Once the consumers reestablished their desired consumption/investment proportions, it is thus revealed that business had invested too much in capital goods and had underinvested in consumer goods. Business had been seduced by the governmental tampering and artificial lowering of the rate of interest, and acted as if more savings were available to invest than were really there. As soon as the new bank money filtered through the system and the consumers reestablished their old proportions, it became clear that there were not enough savings to buy all the producers' goods, and that business had misinvested the limited savings available. Business had overinvested in capital goods and underinvested in consumer products.

The inflationary boom thus leads to distortions of the pricing and production system. Prices of labor and raw materials in the capital goods industries had been bid up during the boom too high to be profitable once the consumers reassert their old consumption/investment preferences. The "depression" is then seen as the necessary and healthy phase by which the market economy sloughs off and liquidates the unsound, uneconomic investments of the boom, and reestablishes those proportions between consumption and investment that are truly desired by the consumers. The depression is the painful but necessary process by which the free market sloughs off the excesses and errors of the boom and reestablishes the market economy in its function of efficient service to the mass of consumers. Since prices of factors of production have been bid too high in the boom, this means that prices of labor and goods in these capital goods industries must be allowed to fall until proper market relations are resumed.

Since the workers receive the increased money in the form of higher wages fairly rapidly, how is it that booms can go on for years without having their unsound investments revealed, their errors due to tampering with market signals become evident, and the depression-adjustment process begins its work? The answer is that booms would be very short lived if the bank credit expansion and subsequent pushing of the rate of interest below the free market level were a one-shot affair. But the point is that the credit expansion is *not* one-shot; it proceeds on and on, never giving consumers the chance to reestablish their preferred proportions of consumption and saving, never allowing the rise in costs in the capital goods industries to catch up to the inflationary rise in prices. Like the repeated doping of a horse, the boom is kept on its way and ahead of its inevitable comeuppance, by repeated doses of the stimulant of bank credit. It is only when bank credit expansion must finally stop, either because the banks are getting into a shaky condition or because the public begins to balk at the continuing inflation, that retribution finally catches up with the boom. As soon as credit expansion stops, then the piper must be paid, and the inevitable readjustments liquidate the unsound over-investments of the boom, with the reassertion of a greater proportionate emphasis on consumers' goods production.

Thus, the Misesian theory of the business cycle accounts for all of our puzzles: The repeated and recurrent nature of the cycle, the massive cluster of entrepreneurial error, the far greater intensity of the boom and bust in the producers' goods industries.

Mises, then, pinpoints the blame for the cycle on inflationary bank credit expansion propelled by the intervention of government and its central bank. What does Mises say should be done, say by government, once the depression arrives? What is the governmental role in the cure of depression? In the first place, government must cease inflating as soon as possible. It is true that this will, inevitably, bring the inflationary boom abruptly to an end, and commence the inevitable recession or depression. But the longer the government waits for this, the worse the necessary readjustments will have to be. The sooner the depression-readjustment is gotten over with, the better. This means, also, that the government must never try to prop up unsound business situations;

it must never bail out or lend money to business firms in trouble. Doing this will simply prolong the agony and convert a sharp and quick depression phase into a lingering and chronic disease. The government must never try to prop up wage rates or prices of producers' goods; doing so will prolong and delay indefinitely the completion of the depression-adjustment process; it will cause indefinite and prolonged depression and mass unemployment in the vital capital goods industries. The government must not try to inflate again, in order to get out of the depression. For even if this reinflation succeeds, it will only sow greater trouble later on. The government must do nothing to encourage consumption, and it must not increase its own expenditures, for this will further increase the social consumption/investment ratio. In fact, cutting the government budget will improve the ratio. What the economy needs is not more consumption spending but more saving, in order to validate some of the excessive investments of the boom.

Thus, what the government should do, according to the Misesian analysis of the depression, is absolutely nothing. It should, from the point of view of economic health and ending the depression as quickly as possible, maintain a strict hands off, "*laissez-faire*" policy. Anything it does will delay and obstruct the adjustment process of the market; the less it does, the more rapidly will the market adjustment process do its work, and sound economic recovery ensue.

The Misesian prescription is thus the exact opposite of the Keynesian: It is for the government to keep absolute hands off the economy and to confine itself to stopping its own inflation and to cutting its own budget.

It has today been completely forgotten, even among economists, that the Misesian explanation and analysis of the depression gained great headway precisely during the Great Depression of the 1930s—the very depression that is always held up to advocates of the free market economy as the greatest single and catastrophic failure of *laissez-faire* capitalism. It was no such thing. 1929 was made inevitable by the vast bank credit expansion throughout the Western world during the 1920s: A policy deliberately adopted by the Western governments, and most importantly by the Federal Reserve System in the United States. It was made possible by the failure of the Western world to return to a genuine gold standard after World War I, and thus allowing more room for inflationary policies by government. Everyone now thinks of President Coolidge as a believer in *laissez-faire* and an unhampered market economy; he was not, and tragically, nowhere less so than in the field of money and credit. Unfortunately, the sins and errors of the Coolidge intervention were laid to the door of a non-existent free market economy.

If Coolidge made 1929 inevitable, it was President Hoover who prolonged and deepened the depression, transforming it from a typically sharp but swiftly-disappearing depression into a lingering and near-fatal malady, a malady "cured" only by the holocaust of World War II. Hoover, not Franklin Roosevelt, was the founder of the policy of the "New Deal": essentially the massive use of the State to do exactly what Misesian theory would most warn against—to prop up wage rates above their free-market levels, prop up prices, inflate credit, and lend money to shaky business positions. Roosevelt only advanced, to a greater degree, what Hoover had pioneered. The result for the first time in American history, was a nearly perpetual depression and nearly permanent mass unemployment. The Coolidge crisis had become the unprecedentedly prolonged Hoover-Roosevelt depression.

Ludwig von Mises had predicted the depression during the heyday of the great boom of the 1920s—a time, just like today, when economists and politicians, armed with a "new economics" of perpetual inflation, and with new "tools" provided by the Federal Reserve System, proclaimed a perpetual "New Era" of permanent prosperity guaranteed by our wise economic doctors in Washington. Ludwig von Mises, alone armed with a correct theory of the business cycle, was one of the very few economists to predict the Great Depression, and hence the economic world was forced to listen to him with respect. F. A. Hayek spread the word in England, and the younger English economists were all, in the early 1930s, beginning to adopt the Misesian cycle theory for their analysis of the depression—and also to adopt, of course, the strictly free-market policy prescription that flowed with this theory. Unfortunately, economists have now adopted the historical notion of Lord Keynes: That no "classical economists" had a theory of the business cycle until Keynes came along in 1936. There *was* a theory of the depression; it was the classical economic tradition; its prescription was strict hard money and *laissez-faire*; and it was rapidly being adopted, in England and even in the United States, as the accepted theory of the business cycle. (A particular irony is that the major "Austrian" proponent in the United States in the early and mid-1930s was none other than Professor Alvin Hansen, very soon to make his mark as the outstanding Keynesian disciple in this country.)

What swamped the growing acceptance of Misesian cycle theory was simply the "Keynesian Revolution"—the amazing sweep that Keynesian theory made of the economic world shortly after the publication of the *General Theory* in 1936. It is not that Misesian theory was refuted successfully; it was just *forgotten* in the rush to climb on the suddenly fashionable Keynesian bandwagon. Some of the leading adherents of the Mises theory—who clearly knew better—succumbed to the newly established winds of doctrine, and won leading American university posts as a consequence.

But now the once arch-Keynesian London *Economist* has recently proclaimed that "Keynes is Dead." After over a decade of facing trenchant theoretical critiques and refutation by stubborn economic facts, the Keynesians are now in general and massive retreat. Once again, the money supply and bank credit are being grudgingly acknowledged to play a leading role in the cycle. The time is ripe—for a rediscovery, a renaissance, of the Mises theory of the business cycle. It can come none too soon; if it ever does, the whole concept of a Council of Economic Advisors would be swept away, and we would see a massive retreat of government from the economic sphere. But for all this to happen, the world of economics, and the public at large, must be made aware of the existence of an explanation of the business cycle that has lain neglected on the shelf for all too many tragic years.

Index

Business cycle
    Austrian, 29, 30, 43
    Keynesian, 9
    Marx, 13
    Ricardian, 21, 28, 29

Central Bank, 27, 28

Coolidge, Calvin, 41, 42

Depression
    as a period of adjustment, 28, 29, 36, 39, 40
    definition of, 8
    following credit expansion, 37, 38, 41
    Great Depression, 40, 43
    length and depth of, 25
    price level during, 29
    prolonged by wage and price rigidity, 39
    theory of, 9, 29, 30

Entrepreneurship, 16

Federal Reserve System, 27, 41, 42

Gold standard, 21, 22, 23, 24, 25, 26, 28, 41

Great Depression
    See Depression

Hayek, F.A.
    Monetary Theory and the Trade Cycle, and *Prices and Production*, 30
        proponent of Austrian business cycle, 30

Hoover, Herbert, 41, 42

Hume, David, 20

Industrial Revolution, 13

Inflation
    causes of, 9
    effects of, 22
    overspending in Keynesian analysis, 9

solutions to, 29
squelched in a competitive banking industry, 26

Interest rate
allocation of resources, 38
manipulation, 31–35
natural, or real, 31–32, 37

Keynes, John Maynard
General Theory of Employment, Interest, and Money, 9
government intervention in the economy, 10

Keynesianism, 9, 43, 44
Keynesian revolution, 44

Laissez-faire policy, 40, 41, 43

Marx, Karl, 13
McCracken, Paul, 10, 11
Mises, Ludwig von, 29, 30, 31, 38, 42, 43, 44, 45
on business cycles, 29
on government intervention during economic crises, 40
on the Great Depression, 40
Theory of Money and Credit, 29

New Deal, 42
Nixon, Richard, 10

Prices
general level of, 14
relative, 25
stabilization, 9
Price theory, 14
Production
time element in, 16

Recession, 8, 9, 10, 17, 38
Ricardo, David, 20
Roosevelt, Franklin Delano, 42

Socialism, 12

Time preference, 31, 34

Unemployment, 11, 39, 42

Wages
government manipulation of, 33, 39
increasing as a result of credit inflation, 33, 42

www.ingramcontent.com/pod-product-compliance
Lightning Source LLC
Chambersburg PA
CBHW061520180526
45171CB00001B/259